FASHION SKETCHING
LE CROQUIS DE MODE
SKETCHING DE MODA

CLAUDIA AUSONIA PALAZIO

promopress

Claudia Ausonia Palazio

Claudia Ausonia Palazio attended the 1st Art Academy in Rome and then obtained a two-year degree from the IED in fashion ('88/'89). She subsequently began working as an assistant costume designer for Bonizza Giordani Aragno, where she had various responsibilities: the design and creation of theatre costumes, staging exhibitions on fashion history (the first, "30 Years of Fashion", for Valentino, and "The Seduction of Craftsmanship", which included a collection of some of the most famous dresses in the history of Italian fashion). In the meantime, she was attending the Accademia di Alta Moda e Arte del costume Koefia ('91/'94), where she graduated with full marks. At the end of her coursework, she was asked to join Koefia's staff, initially teaching as an assistant to the professor of patterns and sketches, and later as an instructor of fashion design. At the same time, she was working as an illustrator for various fashion production companies, jointly participating in television shows as a costume designer. She has been working as a fashion design lecturer since 1996.

This book arose from years teaching at one of the most famous fashion academies in Rome, in which the author noticed the difficulty had by the stylists of the future, who, often lacking artistic training, possessed a limited understanding of human anatomy. Without the fundamental base of the proportions and harmony of the human body, these students were finding it quite difficult to express their incredible creative talents. It is necessary to look to the work of any style and design department to understand how sought out and essential these abilities are, even to the point of representing the very image of a designer. Each style and design department has its own fundamentals that must be renewed year after year to keep up with the pace of fashion. In *Fashion Sketching*, you will find the foundations for women, men and children's clothing that will provide a key, perfect and ready to use immediately by the creative who can then modify the features, hair styles and makeup, according to their personal vision at the time.

Claudia Ausonia Palazio a étudié au premier lycée artistique de Rome puis a passé deux ans à l'IED (Istituto Europeo di Design) en spécialité mode (1988/1989). Elle a commencé à travailler comme couturière assistante pour Bonizza Giordani Aragno et s'est investie dans plusieurs activités : conception et création de costumes pour le théâtre, préparation d'expositions historiques sur la mode (la première fut « 30 ans de mode » pour Valentino, suivie de « La séduction de l'artisanal » qui comprenait une collection de quelques-unes des pièces les plus célèbres de l'histoire de la mode italienne). Dans le même temps, elle suit les cours à l'Accademia di Alta Moda e Arte del Costume Koefia (1991/1994) où elle obtient la note maximale et où, à la fin du cursus, elle est invitée à intégrer le corps enseignant, d'abord comme professeur assistant de création et de dessin de mode puis comme professeur de création de mode. En parallèle, elle réalise des illustrations pour diverses sociétés de création de mode et travaille comme costumière pour des programmes télévisés. Elle est professeure de création de mode depuis 1996.

Claudia Ausonia Palazio frequenta il 1° Liceo Artistico di Roma e successivamente un biennio allo IED indirizzo moda ('88/'89). Inizia a lavorare come assistente costumista per Bonizza Giordani Aragno e svolge diverse attività: disegno e creazione di costumi teatrali, allestimenti di mostre storiche della moda (la prima *30 anni di moda* per Valentino e *La seduzione dell'artigianato* che comprendeva una raccolta di abiti tra i più famosi della storia della moda italiana). Nel frattempo frequenta l'Accademia di Alta Moda e Arte del costume Koefia ('91/'94) dove si diploma con il massimo dei voti e alla fine del corso viene chiamata a far parte dello staff insegnante inizialmente come assistente del professore di disegno/figurino e dal 1996 a tutt'oggi come docente di Fashion Design. Collabora come illustratrice con diverse aziende di produzione moda e a programmi televisivi come costumista.

Claudia Ausonia Palazio asistió al primer Liceo Artístico de Roma y después cursó un bienio en el IED (Istituto Europeo di Design) en la especialidad de Moda (1988/1989). Empezó a trabajar como modista asistente de Bonizza Giordani Aragno y desempeñó diversas actividades: diseño y creación de vestuario teatral, preparación de muestras históricas de la moda (la primera fue «30 años de moda» para Valentino, seguida de «La seducción de lo artesanal», que comprendía una colección de algunos de los vestidos más famosos de la historia de la moda italiana). Al mismo tiempo, asiste a la Accademia di Alta Moda e Arte del Costume Koefia (1991/1994) donde se diploma con la puntuación máxima y, al final del curso, es invitada a formar parte del personal docente, inicialmente como profesora adjunta de diseño y figurines y sucesivamente como docente de Diseño de Moda. Simultáneamente, realiza ilustraciones para diversas empresas de producción de moda y colabora en programas televisivos como responsable del vestuario. En la actualidad es profesora de Diseño de moda desde 1996.

FASHION SKETCHING

TEMPLATES, POSES and IDEAS for FASHION DESIGN

CLAUDIA AUSONIA PALAZIO

LE CROQUIS DE MODE
MODÈLES, POSES & IDÉES pour la CRÉATION de MODE

SKETCHING DE MODA
PLANTILLAS, POSES e IDEAS para el DISEÑO de MODA

promopress

Fashion Sketching:
Templates, Poses and Ideas for Fashion Design

Le croquis de mode:
Modèles, poses & idées pour la création de mode

Sketching de moda:
Plantillas, poses e ideas para el diseño de moda

Original title:
Fashion Silhouette
Pose per la moda da vestire e colorare

Translators:
Katherine Kirby, English translation
Marjorie Gouzée, French translation
Jesús de Cos Pinto, Spanish translation

ISBN English version: 978-84-16504-10-7
ISBN French version: 978-84-16504-43-5
ISBN Spanish version: 978-84-16504-42-8

Copyright © 2016 Ikon Editrice srl – Milano, Italy
Copyright © 2016 Promopress for the English, French
and Spanish language edition

Promopress is a brand of:
Promotora de prensa internacional S.A.
C/ Ausiàs March, 124
08013 Barcelona, Spain
Tel.: 0034 93 245 14 64
Fax: 0034 93 265 48 83
Email: info@promopress.es
www.promopresseditions.com
Facebook: Promopress Editions
Twitter: Promopress Editions @PromopressEd

First published in English, French and Spanish: 2016

Printed in China

FREE ONLINE MATERIALS
Over 200 templates for making your own figures
Get them for free from our website

www.promopresseditions.com/Downloads/Extra free
material using

your promotion code: ZB9WQACCMO

Download the PDF document of the original templates for
the figures featured in the book. You can print and trace the
base templates or export them to digital design programs
and use them with your own fashion designs and creations.

MATÉRIEL GRATUIT EN LIGNE
Plus de 200 bases pour faire vos propres croquis
Téléchargez-les gratuitement sur notre site web

www.promopresseditions.com/Downloads/Extra free
material

avec votre code promo : ZB9WQACCMP

Recevez le PDF des originaux des croquis de ce livre.
Vous pourrez imprimer et calquer les modèles ou encore
les exporter dans des logiciels de dessin numérique et les
utiliser pour habiller et illustrer vos propres créations.

MATERIAL GRATUITO EN LÍNEA
Más de 200 bases para hacer tus propios figurines
Descárgalas gratis en nuestra web

www.promopresseditions.com/Downloads/Extra free
material

con tu código de promoción: ZB9WQACCMN

Consigue el documento PDF con las plantillas originales de
los figurines del libro. Podrás imprimir y calcar las plantillas
de base o exportarlas a programas de diseño digital y
utilizarlas para vestir e ilustrar tus propias creaciones.

CONTENTS
RÉSUMÉ
SOMMARIO
RESUMEN

PREFACE
PRÉFACE
PREFAZIONE
PREFACIO

6—7

INTRODUCTION
INTRODUCTION
INTRODUZIONE
INTRODUCCIÓN

8—15

WOMAN
FEMME
DONNA
MUJER

16—119

CHILD
ENFANT
BIMBO
NIÑO

120—199

MAN
HOMME
UOMO
HOMBRE

200—272

PREFACE

Mario Boselli
Cavaliere del Lavoro
*Honorary President of the Camera
Nazionale della Moda Italiana*

For some time now, training young talent has been a priority for the Camera Nazionale della Moda Italiana (the Chamber of Italian Fashion) which, with particular motivation and effort, has launched special projects and initiatives to offer opportunities of growth, visibility and promotion for emerging designers. In terms of training and education, Italy is at the forefront, with an environment full of foreign students who wish to study the phenomenon of Italian style up close and gain specialised, technical experience.

The book, *Fashion Sketching* was created specifically for students, offering a valid tool to help them practice and learn. One of the strategies that will be helpful to face the current socio-economic crisis and future challenges in foreign markets is that of engaging new generations, focusing on the acquisition of specific skills and abilities that will make a difference for them in the future. Gaining a competitive edge also depends on the quality of the human resources working in companies as well as along the entire fashion supply chain.

Thus, it makes sense to act in a way that the know-how accumulated over the years, best practices and working methodologies can be handed down to the younger generations that are entering this field.

PRÉFACE

Mario Boselli
Cavaliere del Lavoro
*Président honoraire de la Camera
Nazionale della Moda Italiana*

La formation et le soutien des jeunes talents figurent depuis des années parmi les priorités de la Camera Nazionale della Moda Italiana qui, avec beaucoup de motivation et d'engagement, a entrepris des initiatives et projets spéciaux visant à offrir des opportunités de croissance, de visibilité et de promotion aux créateurs émergents. Au niveau de la formation, l'Italie incarne l'excellence et une destination de rêve pour les étudiants étrangers, désireux d'intégrer les écoles de mode italiennes afin d'étudier de près le phénomène de l'*italian style* et d'acquérir une préparation technique et spécialisée.

La publication *Le croquis de mode*, imaginée et pensée spécialement pour les étudiants, constitue un bon outil d'exercice et d'apprentissage. Une des stratégies possibles pour affronter la crise socio-économique actuelle et les défis futurs des marchés étrangers consiste précisément à aider les nouvelles générations à acquérir les aptitudes et compétences spécifiques qui feront la différence. L'obtention d'un avantage compétitif dépend également de la qualité des ressources humaines mises en jeu, tant dans les usines que sur toute la chaîne d'approvisionnement de l'industrie. Il importe donc de s'assurer que les connaissances acquises au fil des années, les bonnes pratiques et la méthodologie puissent être transmises aux nouvelles générations qui émergent dans ce secteur.

PREFAZIONE

Mario Boselli
Cavaliere del Lavoro
*Presidente Onorario della Camera
Nazionale della Moda Italiana*

La formazione e i giovani talenti sono da anni uno degli obiettivi della Camera Nazionale della Moda Italiana che, con forte motivazione e impegno, ha avviato progetti speciali e iniziative per offrire opportunità di crescita, visibilità e promozione ai designer emergenti. Sul fronte della formazione, l'Italia rappresenta un'eccellenza e una meta ambita da studenti stranieri che desiderano entrare nelle scuole di moda italiane dove possono studiare da vicino il fenomeno dell'Italian Style e acquisire una preparazione specializzata e tecnica.

La pubblicazione *Fashion Silhouette*, ideata e pensata *ad hoc* per gli studenti, offre un valido strumento di esercitazione e di apprendimento. Una delle strategie per affrontare l'attuale crisi socio-economica e le future sfide sui mercati esteri è proprio quella di agevolare le nuove generazioni puntando sull'acquisizione di skills e competenze specifiche che faranno la differenza. L'ottenimento di un vantaggio competitivo dipende anche dalla qualità delle risorse umane messe in campo sia nelle aziende che lungo tutta la catena di fornitura della filiera.

Occorre quindi fare in modo che il know-how acquisito negli anni, le buone prassi e la metodologia di lavoro possano essere trasferite alle nuove generazioni che si affacciano su questo settore.

PREFACIO

Mario Boselli
Cavaliere del Lavoro
*Presidente honorario de la Camera
Nazionale della Moda Italiana*

La formación y el apoyo a los jóvenes talentos se cuenta desde hace años entre las prioridades de la Camera Nazionale della Moda Italiana que, con gran motivación y empeño, ha iniciado proyectos especiales e iniciativas para ofrecer oportunidades de crecimiento, visibilidad y promoción a los diseñadores emergentes. En el terreno de la formación, Italia representa la excelencia y es una meta deseada por los estudiantes extranjeros, que desean entrar en las escuelas de moda italiana para estudiar de cerca el fenómeno del *italian style* y adquirir una preparación técnica y especializada.

La publicación *Sketching de moda*, ideada y pensada especialmente para los estudiantes, ofrece un instrumento válido de ejercicio y de aprendizaje. Una de las estrategias para afrontar la actual crisis socioeconómica y los retos futuros de los mercados extranjeros es precisamente ayudar a las nuevas generaciones a adquirir las aptitudes y las competencias específicas que marcarán la diferencia. La obtención de una ventaja competitiva depende también de la calidad de los recursos humanos que se pongan en juego, tanto en las fábricas como en toda la cadena de suministros a la industria. Por ello, es preciso actuar de manera que los conocimientos adquiridos con los años, las buenas prácticas y la metodología del trabajo puedan ser transferidos a las nuevas generaciones que emergen en este sector.

INTRODUCTION

Since ancient times, clothes have been depicted in sketches, though they may vary in detail. We can even find images of the sort going back 5,000 years ago in aboriginal art or in Egyptian stencils, up to the famous bikini-clad women of Piazza Armerina in Sicily. People felt the need to depict stylised human figures in order to leave a trace of their own customs and culture, explaining why we often find images of hunts, festivals and divinities. For us today, these designs embody the history of our earth and, despite using different techniques, we continue to represent our modern times—often through a pencil. Drawing a human figure, however, is not as easy as it may seem; one must first have a "good eye" and "a hand" for properly capturing the right proportions of a real, three dimensional figure and transforming it onto a two dimensional surface: a piece of paper. A line misplaced only by a millimetre can make our sketch look out of proportion. Fashion academies teach students to create a drawing, or base, or sketch as it is often called, but not all designers manage to recreate them after graduation without the assistance of their instructors. Hence they find themselves going for years, creating designs upon the same base without being able to advance their looks. For a designer, renewal is fundamental, or else he risks that his work will go out of style - a new sketch can act as a stimulus for the creation of new lines.

This book is directed at our designers, be they aspiring, students or already working for a fashion house, as they represent the often-neglected human figure, which we call the "sketch".

How to use a sketch

To make the best use of the fundamentals set forth in this book, we recommend purchasing an overhead projector or a light table. Place the blank paper over the base, which will appear as a transparency. The first few times, you can trace the entire sketch directly, then afterwards lighten the outline with a putty rubber and proceed to drawing the outfit. However, the best way to use these sketches, which we particularly endorse, is to place the blank paper on top of the base, then immediately start drawing the clothing. Then, if you like the silhouette, you can finish by drawing only the part of the sketch that emerges from the clothing, thereby avoiding the weight of the erased portions. In this book, you will find a few examples of how the bases that we supply can be used.

A word on colour techniques

There are various types of fashion drawings, but two main ones are:
— The sketch, which represents a stylised outfit, but one that is perfectly understandable in terms of a pattern, fundamental for a company when presenting an entire collection. The sketch is like a blueprint;
— An illustration, which represents an already existing item of clothing and which often is seen in fashion magazines or decorating *ateliers*. They're flashes of a vision that demonstrate the essence of the look.

Colouring a sketch

We recommend using 80 gram A4 copy or printer paper. Begin by drawing the dress with a .5 or .7 mm mechanical pencil (we recommend B or 2B for the precision of the line it makes). Then erase the sketch with a putty rubber and colour the image with Pantone professional markers, also making use of soft pastels to create chiaroscuro effects and texture details. Finally, you can use a technical pen or a biro, or even a pencil, to recreate the lines of the drawing. You can also use differently coloured gel pens to create fabrics, prints or other details. In addition, if the drawing features a clearly defined outline, you can use computer programs to add colour to the sketch, such as Photoshop and Illustrator, which simplify the creation of patterns, prints, lace and fabric weaves in particular, and which are often used to create backgrounds.

Colouring an illustration
This is a much more varied topic, starting from the paper that, though not necessarily white, must always be high quality. You can use murillo, sketch paper or cardboard based papers of various types and colours including straw paper, depending on the technique you intend to employ. For example, if you use tempera, acrylic or watercolour, it's necessary to also use a type of paper that can appropriately absorb water. The drawing can be done in a thick 6B pencil for example, or even with coloured pencil, charcoal or pen and ink—in short, the illustration is meant to be creative and mixing techniques is encouraged, be they watercolour and pastel, gouache and nib, and so on. It's an instinctive process and should present the essence of your idea. With this type of illustration it is also possible to make use of computer programs. Each designer must find his own personal style of artistic representation, and it's necessary to establish these fundamentals in order to best communicate personal creativity—which is, after all, the purpose of the book.

The author

INTRODUCTION

Depuis l'Antiquité, les articles d'habillement ont été représentés sur des silhouettes plus ou moins précises. Ainsi, l'art primitif dévoile des images de ce type qui datent de 5000 ans, et le vêtement est également présent dans les peintures égyptiennes ou sur les célèbres femmes en bikini de la piazza Armerina. La représentation de figures humaines stylisées était indispensable pour laisser une trace des us et coutumes, et c'est la raison pour laquelle l'Antiquité nous a légué des images de chasses, de fêtes et de divinités.

Ces dessins constituent l'histoire du monde et, si les techniques varient, nous continuons de représenter notre époque à coup de crayon. Cependant, dessiner une silhouette humaine n'est pas si simple qu'il y paraît : cela demande avant tout d'avoir l'*œil* et le *tracé* pour capter les proportions exactes d'une image réelle en trois dimensions et la transférer en deux dimensions, celles de la feuille. Une ligne déplacée ne serait-ce que d'un millimètre peut produire une sensation de déséquilibre. Les universités de mode apprennent à créer une silhouette, base ou modèle, comme on les appelle, mais tous les stylistes ne parviennent pas pour autant à les reproduire sans la correction de leurs professeurs. Ils passent ainsi des années à dessiner toujours sur les mêmes bases, sans parvenir à renouveler leur propre style. Or, pour un styliste, il est essentiel de se renouveler, puisqu'il court sans cesse le risque que son travail « passe de mode » et qu'une silhouette neuve serve d'inspiration pour créer une nouvelle ligne. Cet ouvrage est dédié précisément aux stylistes, qu'il s'agisse de débutants, d'étudiants ou professionnels en poste, et il vise à les aider à représenter ce type si élaboré de figure humaine que nous appelons croquis.

Comment utiliser les croquis

Pour tirer le meilleur parti des croquis présentés dans cet ouvrage, le mieux est de s'équiper d'une table lumineuse ou d'une table en verre avec une lampe en dessous. En plaçant une feuille blanche par-dessus le croquis, vous verrez celui-ci par transparence. Les premières fois, vous pouvez décalquer le dessin en entier puis alléger les traits avec une gomme et dessiner le vêtement. Toutefois le meilleur système, que nous conseillons, consiste à mettre la feuille blanche au-dessus du modèle, à dessiner le vêtement directement et ensuite, si le dessin vous plaît, à terminer en ne traçant que les parties de la silhouette qui dépassent, pour éviter les efforts inutiles. Le livre explique comment tirer profit des croquis que nous présentons.

Conseils pour les techniques de couleur

Il existe plusieurs types de dessins de mode, mais les deux fondamentaux sont :

— le croquis, qui représente un vêtement stylisé, mais parfaitement compréhensible du point de vue du modèle. C'est un élément fondamental des sociétés de mode pour la présentation de collections complètes. Le croquis constitue le projet ;
— le dessin d'illustration, qui présente le vêtement déjà existant et que nous voyons souvent dans les revues de mode ou collé dans l'atelier. Ce sont des dessins de type esquisse, qui montrent l'essence du modèle.

Coloration des croquis

Je conseille de choisir du papier de photocopie ou d'imprimante de 80 g/m^2, format A4. On commence par dessiner le vêtement avec un crayon à mine fine, de 0,5 ou 0,7 mm, dureté B à 2B pour la précision du trait. Ensuite, on gomme le dessin avec une gomme souple, on colorie avec des Pantone (feutres professionnels) et on se sert de pastels mous pour créer des clairs-obscurs et des détails. Enfin, on peut utiliser un rotring ou un stylo, ou encore le même crayon, pour repasser sur les traits du dessin. On utilise également des stylos à encre gel de plusieurs couleurs pour créer des tissus, des imprimés, etc. Si le contour du dessin est bien net, le modèle peut également être colorié à l'aide de programmes informatiques comme Photoshop et Illustrator, qui simplifient surtout la création de tissus à imprimés, à dentelle et à trame et qui sont également utiles pour la création de fonds.

Coloration des illustrations

ici les options sont beaucoup plus nombreuses, à commencer par le papier qui doit être de qualité, mais qui ne doit pas nécessairement être blanc. On peut utiliser du papier bristol Murillo ou du papier à dessin, mais également des papiers cartonnés de divers types et couleurs, et même du papier paille, selon la technique que l'on souhaite adopter. Par exemple, pour de la gouache, de l'acrylique ou de l'aquarelle, nous aurons besoin d'un papier adapté pour absorber l'eau. Nous pouvons dessiner avec un crayon gras 6B ou avec de la sanguine ou du fusain, mais aussi directement avec de l'encre de Chine et une plume. En résumé, le dessin d'illustration est créatif et nous conseillons de mélanger les techniques : aquarelle et pastel, gouache et plume, etc. C'est un art instinctif qui doit transmettre l'essence d'une idée. Il est également possible d'employer des programmes informatiques pour ce type de dessins. Chacun doit trouver son style et il sera primordial de s'approprier ces modèles pour communiquer au maximum sa créativité personnelle. Voilà l'objectif de ce livre.

L'auteure

INTRODUZIONE

Fin dall'antichità gli abiti erano raffigurati su silhouettes, più o meno precise, possiamo già trovare immagini del genere 5000 anni fa nell'arte aborigena, o negli stencil egiziani, fino alle famosissime donne in bikini di piazza Armerina. Nasceva l'esigenza di disegnare figure umane stilizzate per lasciare traccia dei propri usi e costumi, infatti spesso nell'antichità troviamo immagini di caccia, di feste, di divinità.

Questi disegni sono oggi, per noi, la storia della nostra terra e seppur con tecniche diverse, continuiamo a rappresentare i nostri tempi usando la matita. Disegnare una figura umana, però, non è così semplice come può sembrare, bisogna innanzitutto avere "occhio e mano" per saper cogliere le giuste proporzioni da un'immagine reale a tre dimensioni per riportarla alle due dimensioni del foglio. Una linea spostata di un solo millimetro può dare alla nostra silhouette un'idea di sproporzione. Le Accademie di Moda insegnano a creare una silhouette, o base, o figurino come spesso viene chiamata, ma non tutti gli stilisti, dopo il diploma riescono a riprodurne di nuove, senza le correzioni dei loro insegnanti. E si ritrovano per anni a disegnare sempre sulle stesse basi, senza riuscire a rinnovare il proprio stile. Per uno stilista è fondamentale rinnovarsi, poiché rischia ogni giorno che il suo operato non sia più "di moda" e una nuova silhouette serve da stimolo per creare nuove linee.

Questo libro è indirizzato proprio ai nostri stilisti, che essi siano aspiranti, studenti o lavorino già in azienda, perché possa essere di aiuto nel rappresentare questa figura umana, tanto sofferta, che noi chiamiamo silhouette.

Come usare la silhouette

Per sfruttare al meglio le basi proposte in questo libro consigliamo di munirsi di una lavagna luminosa, o un tavolo di vetro con una luce sotto. Poggiando il foglio bianco sulla base la vedremo in trasparenza, le prime volte possiamo ricalcare per intero la silhouette, dopodiché alleggerite il tratto con una gomma pane e procedete nel disegno dell'abito. Ma il modo migliore, quello da noi consigliato, è quello di appoggiare il foglio bianco sulla base, cominciare direttamente a disegnare l'abito e dopo, se il disegno ci piace, possiamo concludere disegnando solo la parte della silhouette che fuoriesce dai vestiti, eliminando le cancellature. Nel libro presentiamo esempi di come può essere sfruttata ogni base che vi proponiamo.

Consigli sulle tecniche di colore

Ci sono diverse tipologie di disegno nella moda, quelle fondamentali sono due:
— *il figurino*, che rappresenta un abito stilizzato ma perfettamente comprensibile modellisticamente, fondamentale nelle aziende per la presentazione di intere collezioni. Il figurino è il progetto;
— *il disegno di illustrazione*, che va a rappresentare l'abito già esistente, e che spesso vediamo nelle riviste di moda, o appeso negli atelier. Sono disegni schizzati, che mostrano l'essenza del look.

Per colorare un figurino

Consiglio una carta per fotocopie o da stampante da 80 gr, formato A4. Si comincia con il disegnare l'abito con una matita micromina 0,5 o 0,7, mina da B a 2B, per la precisione del suo tratto, dopo si sgomma il disegno con una gomma pane e si colora con marker professionali, usare poi pastelli morbidi per creare chiaroscuri e trame particolari. Infine si può usare o la penna tecnica o una biro, oppure di nuovo la matita, per ricreare il tratto del disegno. Si possono usare anche penne gel di vari colori per creare tessuti, stampe o altro. Inoltre se il tratto del disegno è già ben chiuso all'esterno, si possono utilizzare programmi informatici per la colorazione del figurino, quali Photoshop e Illustrator, che semplificano soprattutto la creazione di tessuti stampati, pizzo e trame, molto usati anche per la creazione di sfondi.

Per colorare un'illustrazione

Qui l'argomento è molto più vasto, cominciando dalla carta che deve essere di qualità e non sempre bianca. Si può usare un murillo, una carta da spolvero, ma anche cartoncini di vario tipo e vari colori compresa la cartapaglia, dipende dalla tecnica che si intende usare; per esempio se usiamo tempere, acrilici o acquerelli procuratevi un foglio adatto a ricevere l'acqua. Il disegno si può fare con una matita grassa tipo 6B oppure con una sanguigna o un carboncino, ma anche con china e pennino, insomma il disegno di illustrazione è creativo ed è consigliato mischiare le tecniche; acquerello e pastelli, gouache e pennino e così via; un disegno istintivo deve trasmettere l'essenza della vostra idea. Anche per questo tipo di disegno è possibile l'utilizzo di programmi informatici. Ognuno deve trovare il suo stile di rappresentazione, bisogna fare proprie queste basi, per poter comunicare al meglio la propria creatività.

L'autore

INTRODUCCIÓN

Desde la antigüedad, las prendas de vestir se han representado con siluetas más o menos precisas; en el arte primitivo hay imágenes de este tipo que datan de hace 5.000 años, y la indumentaria está también presente en las pinturas egipcias o en las famosas mujeres en bikini de la piazza Armerina. Existía la necesidad de representar figuras humanas estilizadas para dejar constancia de los usos y costumbres propios, y es por ello que la antiguedad nos ha legado imágenes de caza, de fiestas y de divinidades.

Estos dibujos representan la historia del mundo y, aunque con técnicas distintas, continuamos representando nuestro tiempo mediante el lápiz.

Sin embargo, dibujar una figura humana no es algo tan sencillo como pueda parecer: requiere, ante todo, tener el *ojo* y la *mano* para saber captar las justas proporciones de una imagen real en tres dimensionas y convertirlas en otra en dos dimensiones, las de la hoja. Una línea desplazada aunque sólo sea un milímetro puede producir una sensación de desproporción en la silueta. Las academias de moda enseñan a crear una silueta, base o figurín, como se les suele llamar, pero no todos los estilistas consiguen reproducirlos después sin la corrección de los profesores. De ahí que se dediquen durante años a diseñar siempre sobre las mismas bases, sin conseguir renovar su propio estilo. Para un estilista es fundamental renovarse: dado que a diario corre el riesgo de que su trabajo "pase de moda", una silueta nueva sirve de estímulo para crear una línea nueva.

Este libro está dirigido precisamente a los estilistas, ya se trate de aspirantes, de estudiantes o de profesionales en activo, y su finalidad es ayudarles a representar este tipo tan elaborado de figura humana que llamamos figurín.

Cómo utilizar los figurines

Para sacar el mejor partido de los figurines presentados en este libro, es conveniente proveerse de una mesa de luz o de una mesa con tablero de cristal con una luz debajo. Al colocar una hoja en blanco encima del figurín, veremos éste por transparencia; las primeras veces podemos calcar el figurín por completo y después aligerar los trazos con una goma de borrar y proceder a diseñar la prenda. Pero el mejor sistema, el que aconsejamos, es poner la hoja blanca encima del figurín, empezar a dibujar la prenda directamente y después, si el diseño nos gusta, terminar dibujando sólo las partes de la silueta que sobresalen de las ropas, evitando así la pesadez del borrado. En el libro hay algunos ejemplos de cómo se pueden aprovechar los figurines que presentamos.

Consejos sobre técnicas de coloreado

Hay varios tipos de dibujos de moda, pero los dos fundamentales son:

— el figurín, que representa una prenda estilizada pero perfectamente comprensible desde el punto de vista del patronaje; es un elemento fundamental en las empresas de moda para la presentación de colecciones completas. El figurín es el proyecto;

— el dibujo de ilustración, que representa la prenda ya existente y que vemos a menudo en las revistas de moda o colgados en el taller. Son dibujos tipo boceto, que muestran la esencia del modelo.

Coloreado de figurines

Aconsejo usar papel de fotocopias o de impresora de 80 g/m², formato A4. Se empieza dibujando la prenda con un lápiz de mina fina, de 0,5 o 0,7 mm, de dureza B a 2B por la precisión de su trazo; después, se borra el dibujo con una goma moldeable y se colorea con Pantone (rotuladores profesionales), y se emplean pasteles blandos para crear claroscuros y tramas de detalle. Finalmente, se puede usar un rotring o un bolígrafo, o incluso el mismo lápiz, para repasar los trazos del dibujo. También se utilizan bolígrafos de tinta gel de varios colores para crear tejidos, estampados, etc. Por otra parte, si el contorno exterior del diseño está bien cerrado, el figurín puede colorearse con programas informáticos como Photoshop e Illustrator, que simplifican sobre todo la creación de tejidos estampados, encajes y tramas, y también son muy útiles para la creación de fondos.

Coloreado de ilustraciones

Aquí las opciones son mucho más variadas, empezando por el papel, que debe ser de calidad y no necesariamente blanco. Se pueden usar cartulina Murillo o cartón para frescos, pero también cartulinas de diversos tipos y colores, y hasta papel de salvamanteles, todo depende de la técnica que se quiera aplicar; por ejemplo, si usamos colores de témpera, acrílicos o acuarelas necesitaremos un papel adecuado para recibir el agua. El dibujo se puede hacer con un lápiz graso 6B o con sanguina o carboncillo, pero también directamente con tinta china y plumilla. En suma, el dibujo de ilustraciones es creativo y se aconseja mezclar las técnicas: acuarela y pastel, guache y pluma, etc.; es un arte instintivo y debe transmitir la esencia de una idea. También para este tipo de dibujo es posible emplear programas informáticos. Cada cual debe buscar su estilo de representación, y será preciso apropiarse de estos figurines para comunicar al máximo la creatividad personal. Éste es el objetivo del libro.

La autora

1   2   3

How to use the sketch

1. Lay a white sheet of paper over the sketch. Trace the figure with a hard pencil (such as 2H), then draw the clothing with a slightly softer propelling pencil (such as 2B).
2. Go over the clothing again with the 2B propelling pencil, erasing the parts of the figure which are covered up by the clothes.
3. Start colouring the sketch with Pantone markers.
4. Once you're done with the Pantone markers, wait 20 seconds for the ink to dry, then go over the parts where you would like there to be a bit of shadow (folds, draping, etc.) a second time.
5. Use the pastels to create chiaroscuro effects and add makeup and texture to the fabrics.
6. Lastly, add details with technical pens in various sizes and coloured gel pens.

Comment utiliser les modèles

1. Posez une feuille blanche sur la silhouette et décalquez-la avec un crayon dur de type 2H. Ensuite, esquissez le vêtement avec un porte-mine plus gras, de type 2B.
2. Repassez sur le tracé du vêtement avec la mine 2B et gommez les parties de la silhouette censées être couvertes.
3. Coloriez avec un feutre Pantone.
4. Laissez sécher le Pantone une vingtaine de secondes. Ensuite, repassez au feutre sur les zones d'ombre (plis, drapés, etc.).
5. Utilisez des pastels de couleur pour créer les effets d'ombre et de lumière, les qualités et trames des tissus.
6. Enfin, fignolez les détails avec des stylos Rotring ou du même genre, de différentes épaisseurs, et avec des stylos à encre gel de couleur.

4   5   6

Come usare la silhouette

1. Sovrapporre un foglio bianco sulla silhouette e ricalcarla con una matita dura tipo 2H, poi accennare l'abito con una matita micromina più grossa tipo 2B.

2. Ripassare con micromina 2B il disegno dell'abito cancellando le parti della silhouette che vengono coperte.

3. Iniziare la colorazione usando un Pantone.

4. Una volta passato il Pantone, aspettare 20 secondi che si asciughi e ripassarlo nei punti dove vogliamo l'ombra (pieghe, drappeggi ecc.

5. Usare i pastelli per creare effetti di luci e ombre e per creare trucco e trama di tessuti.

6. Infine curare i particolari con rapidograph di varie misure e penne gel colorate.

Cómo utilizar las siluetas

1. Pon un folio blanco encima de la silueta y cálcala con un lápiz duro tipo 2H. Después, aboceta el vestido con un portaminas con una mina más gruesa, tipo 2B.

2. Repasa el dibujo de la ropa con el portaminas con mina 2B y cubre las partes de la silueta que deban quedar tapadas.

3. Empieza a colorear con un rotulador Pantone.

4. Deja secar el Pantone unos veinte segundos. A continuación, repásalo en las zonas que vayan a ir sombreadas (pliegues, drapeados, etc.).

5. Utiliza colores pastel para crear los efectos de luces y sombras y las calidades y tramas de los tejidos.

6. Por último, pule los detalles con estilógrafos Rotring o similares de varios grosores y con rotuladores gel de colores.

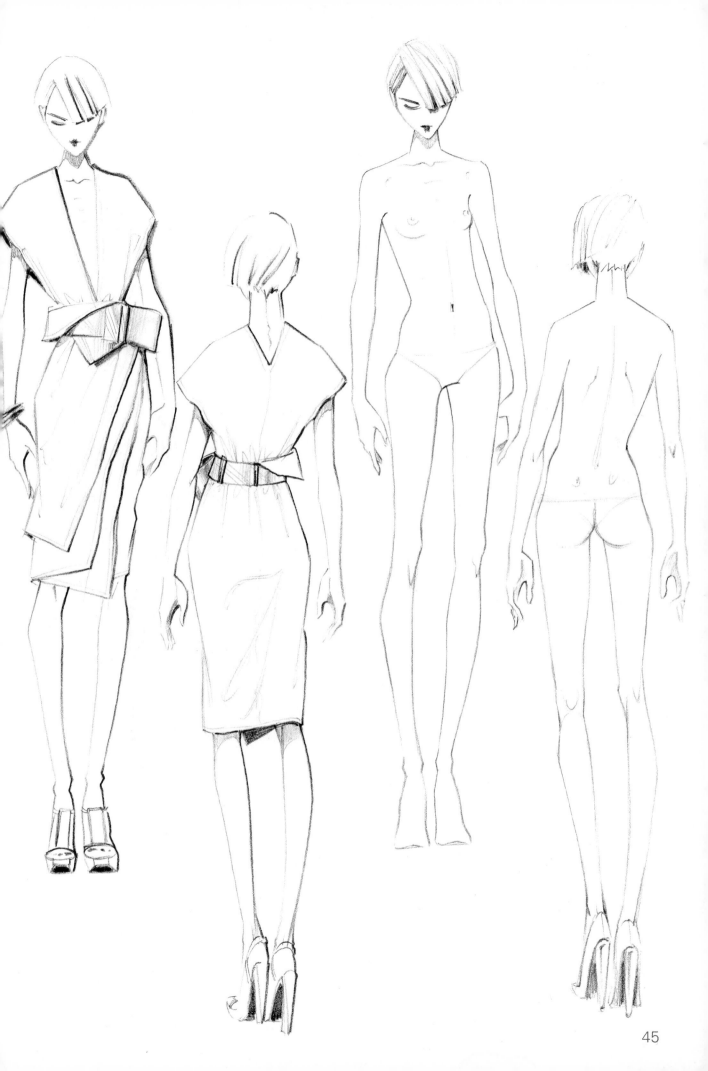

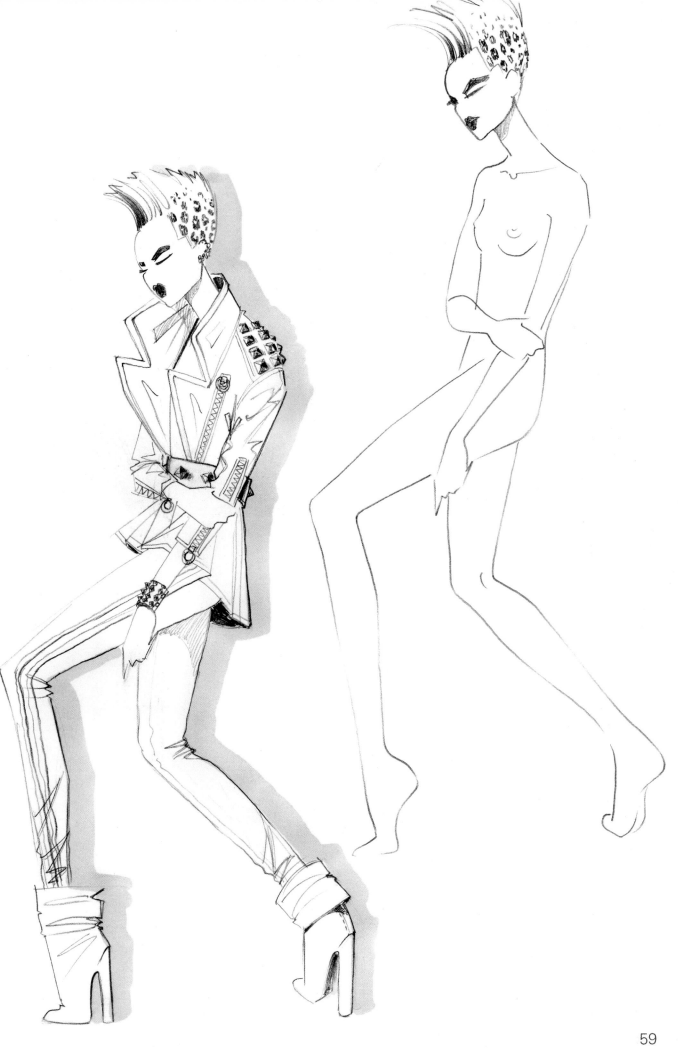

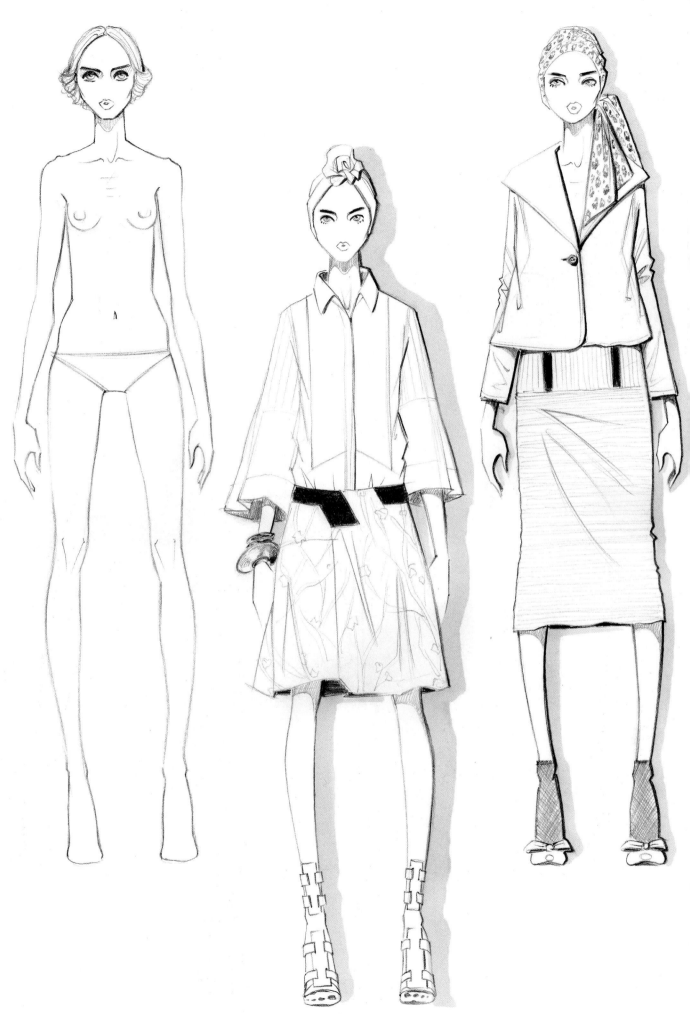

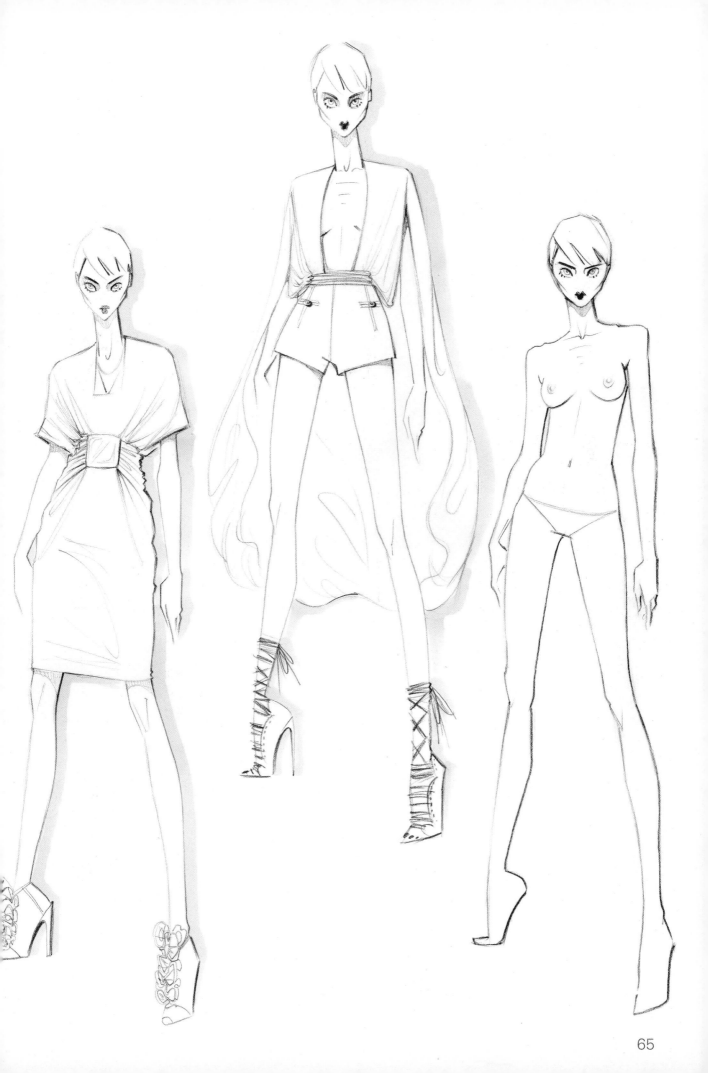

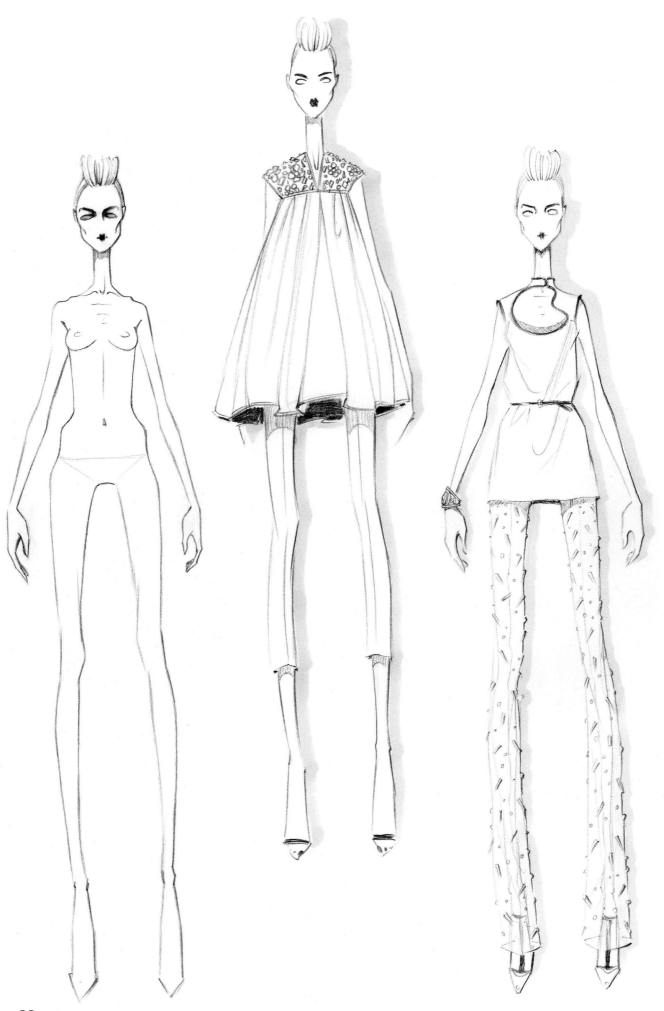

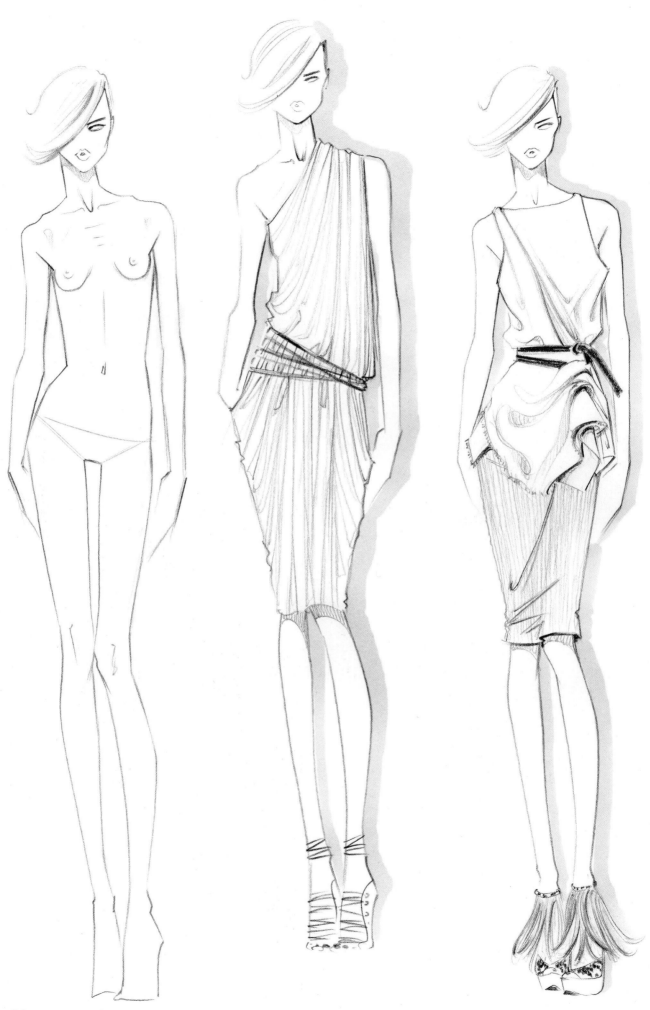

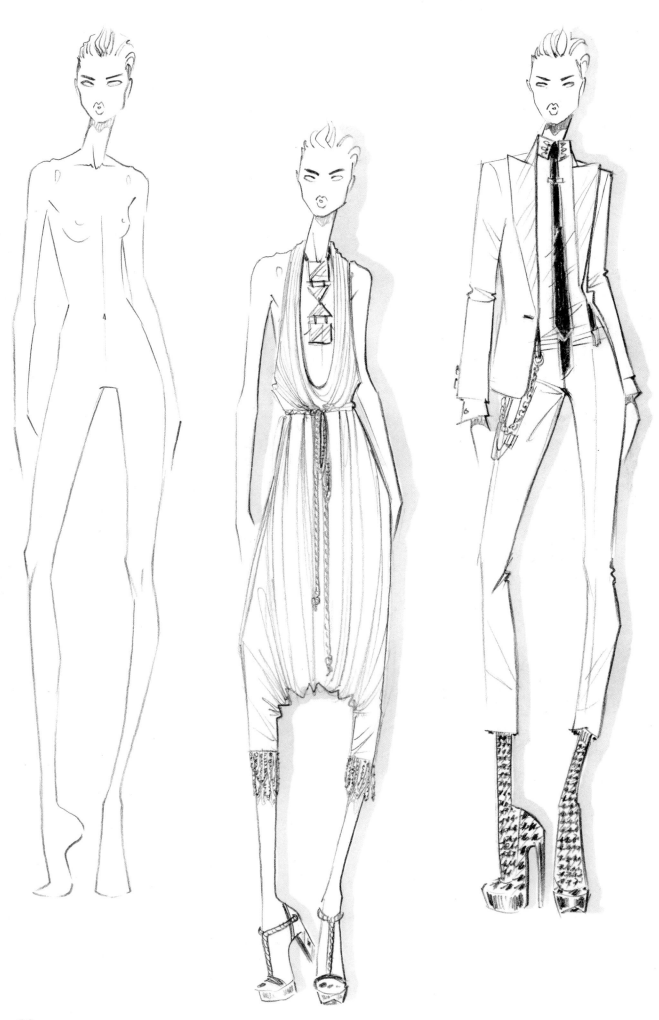

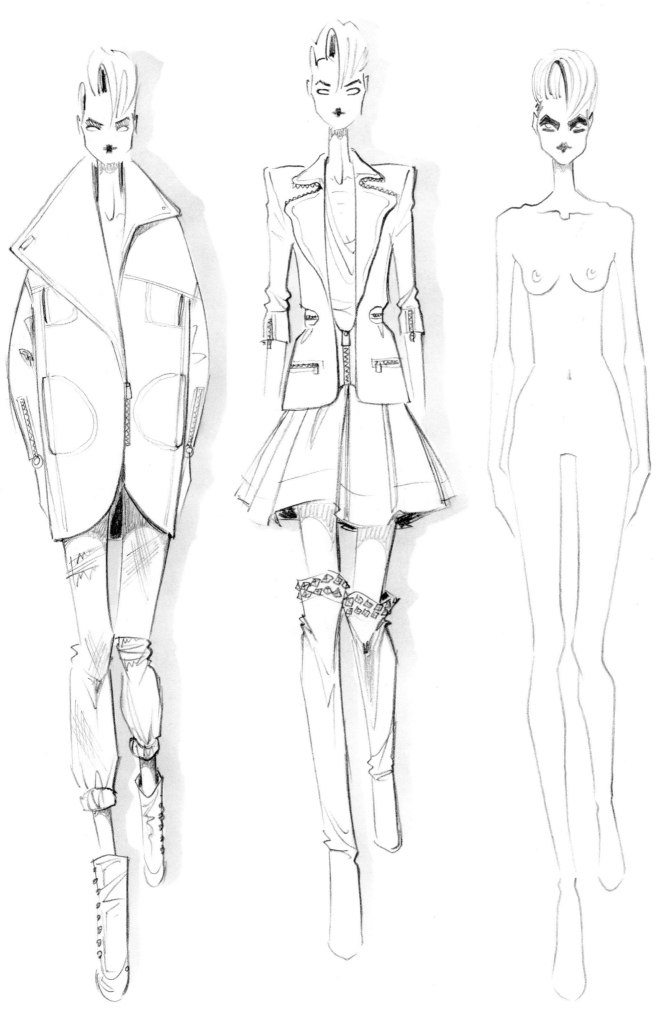

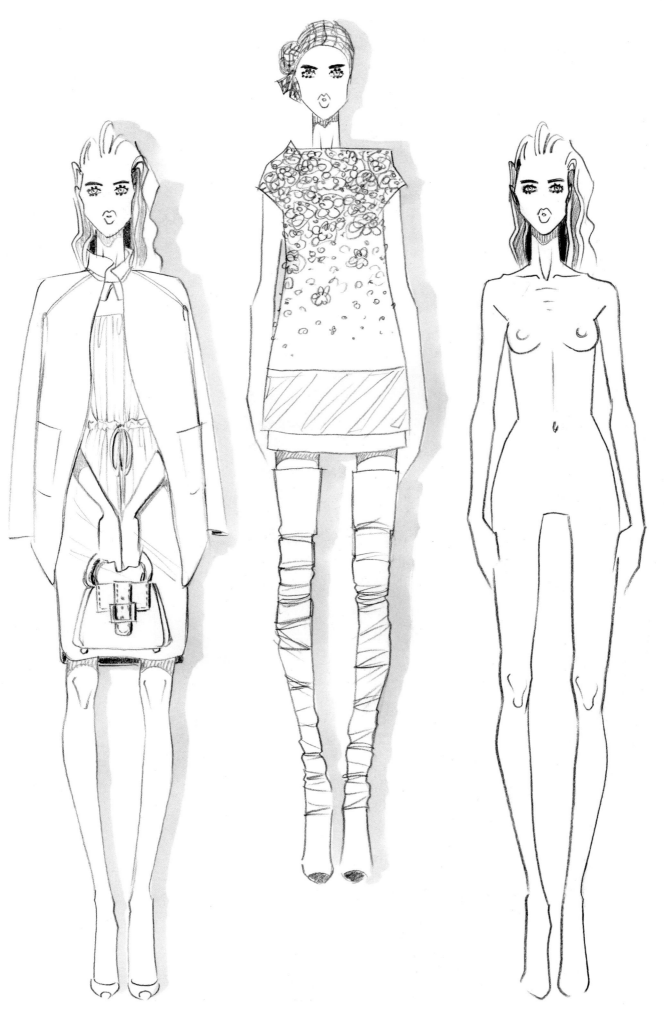

P. 50
P. 79

P. 46   P. 97   P. 97

109

P. 42

P. 41

P. 86

P. 89

P. 72

P. 98

P. 91

P. 47

P. 18

P. 60

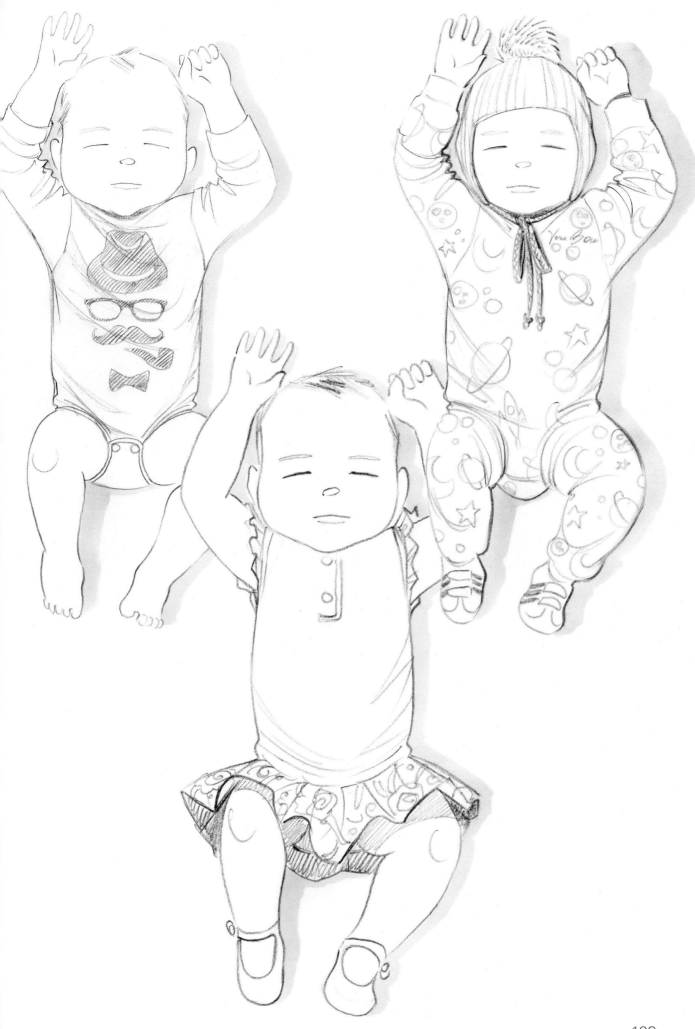

12 m.

18 m.

135

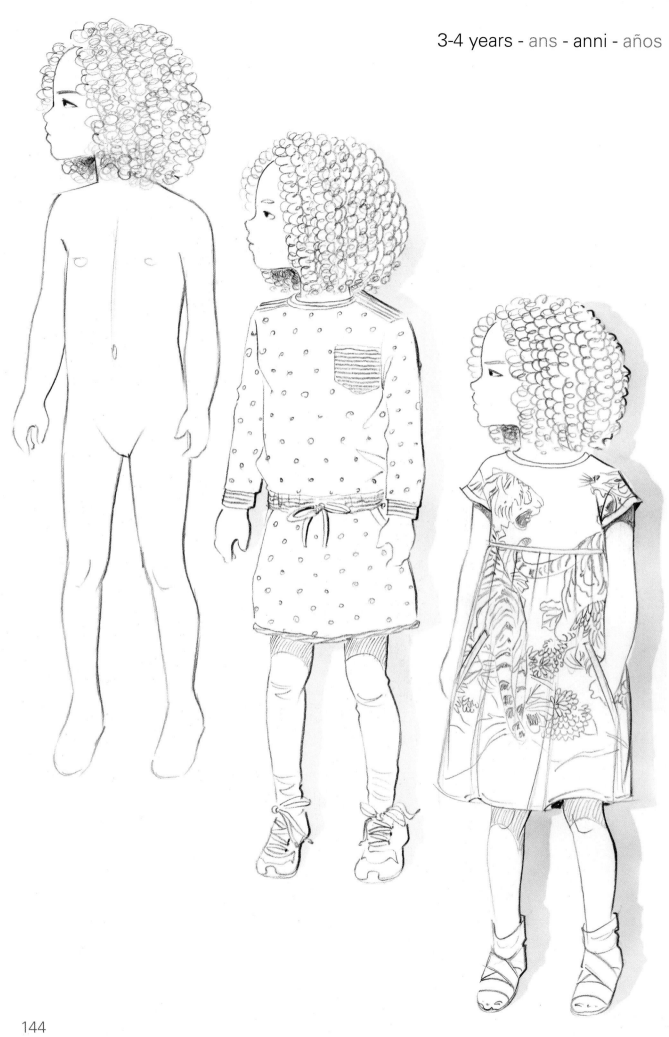

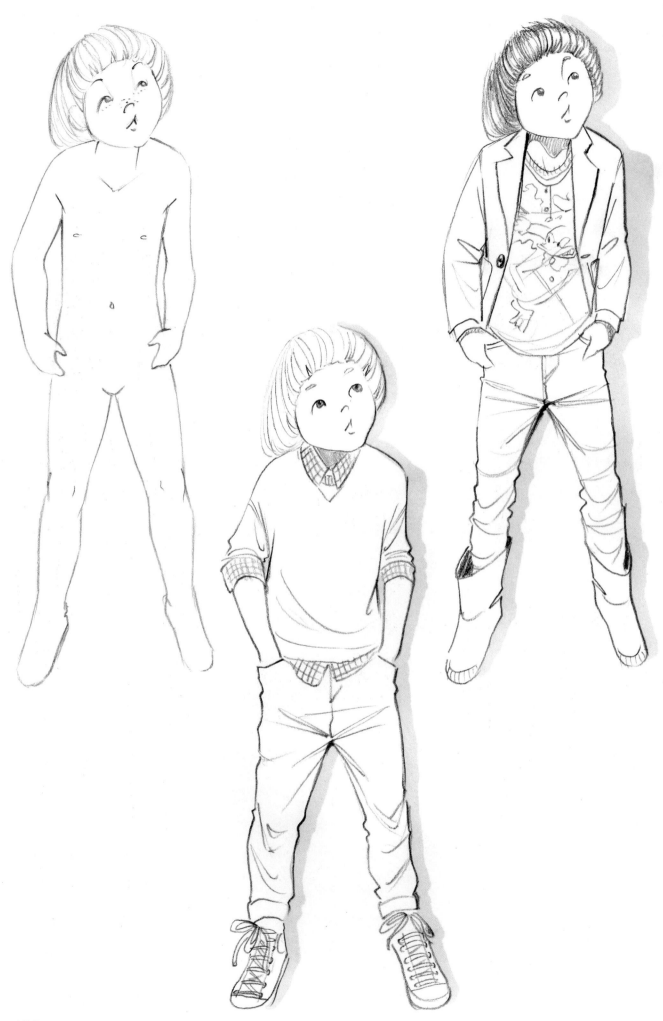

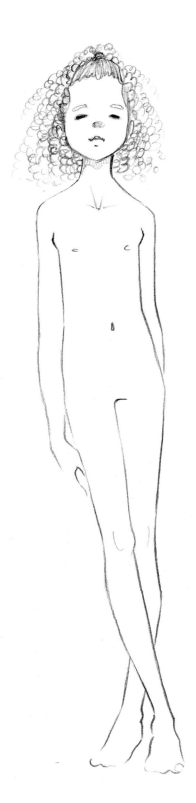

182

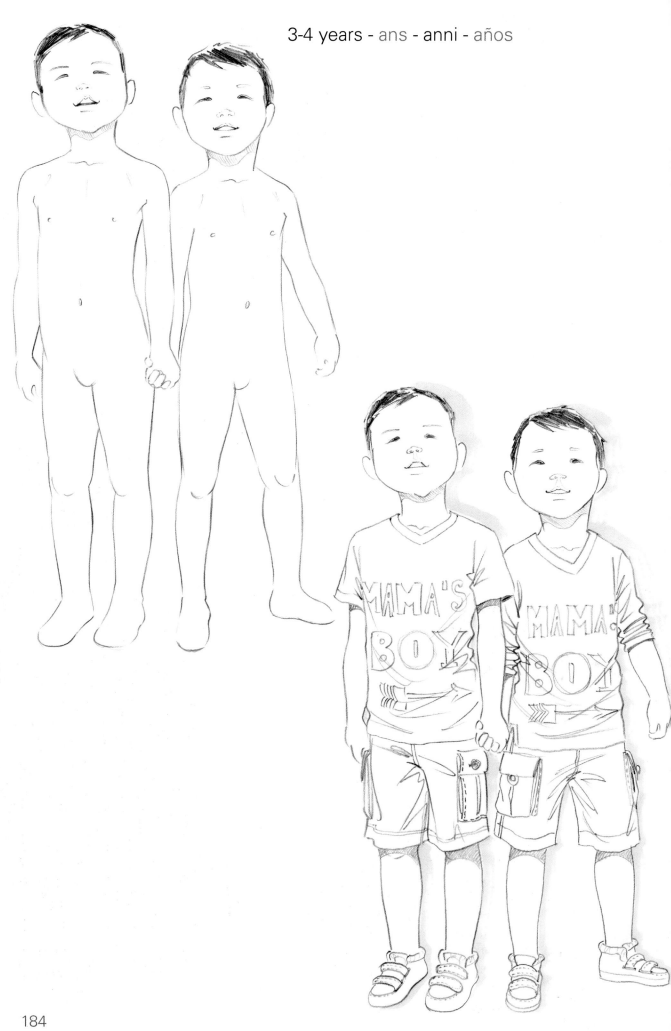

P. 124

P. 123

P. 132

P. 133

185

P. 135

P. 140

P. 143

P. 177

P. 153

P. 165

P. 174

P. 163

P. 181

P. 166

P. 170

P. 162

P. 165

P. 154

P. 141

P. 144

P. 146

P. 147

P. 148

P. 173   P. 167

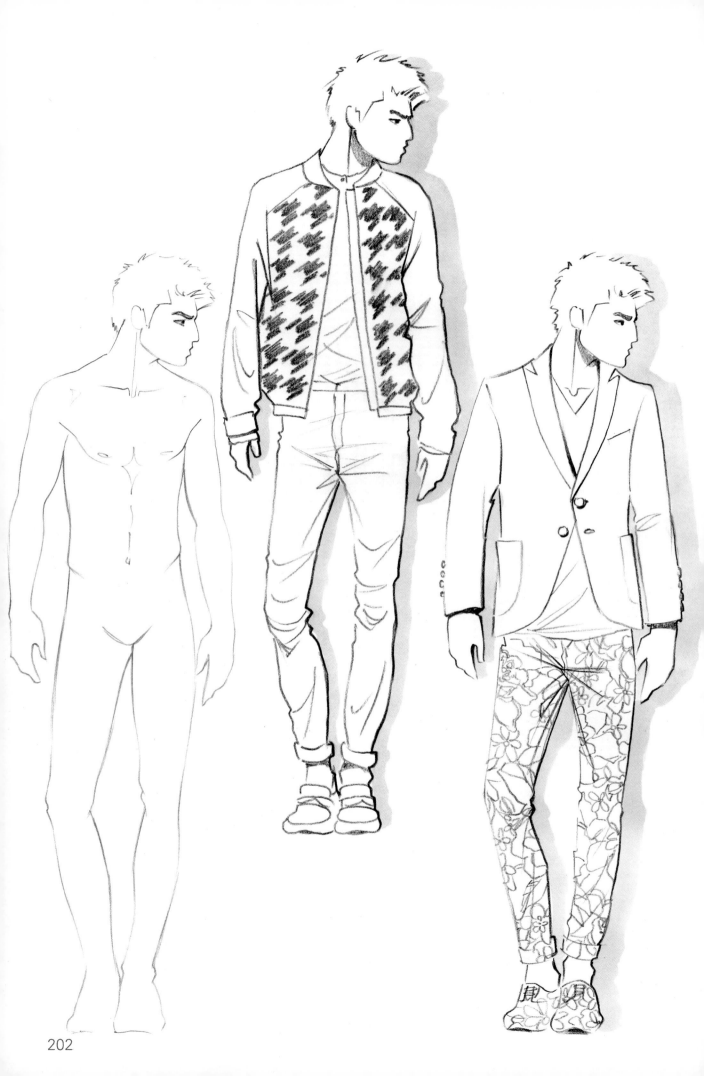

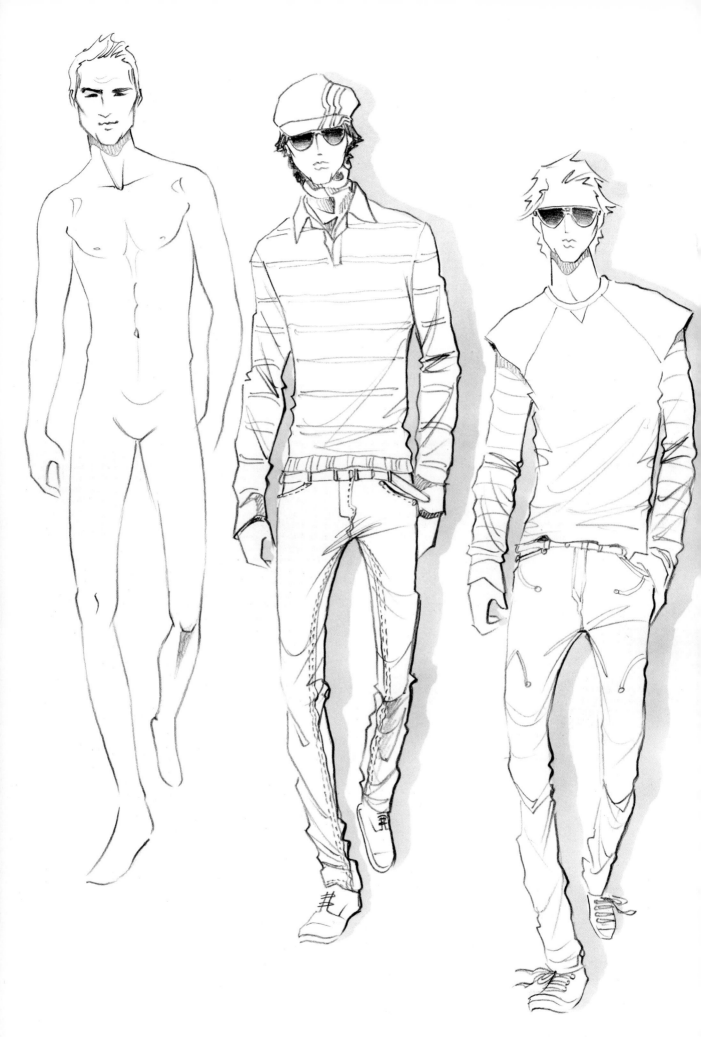

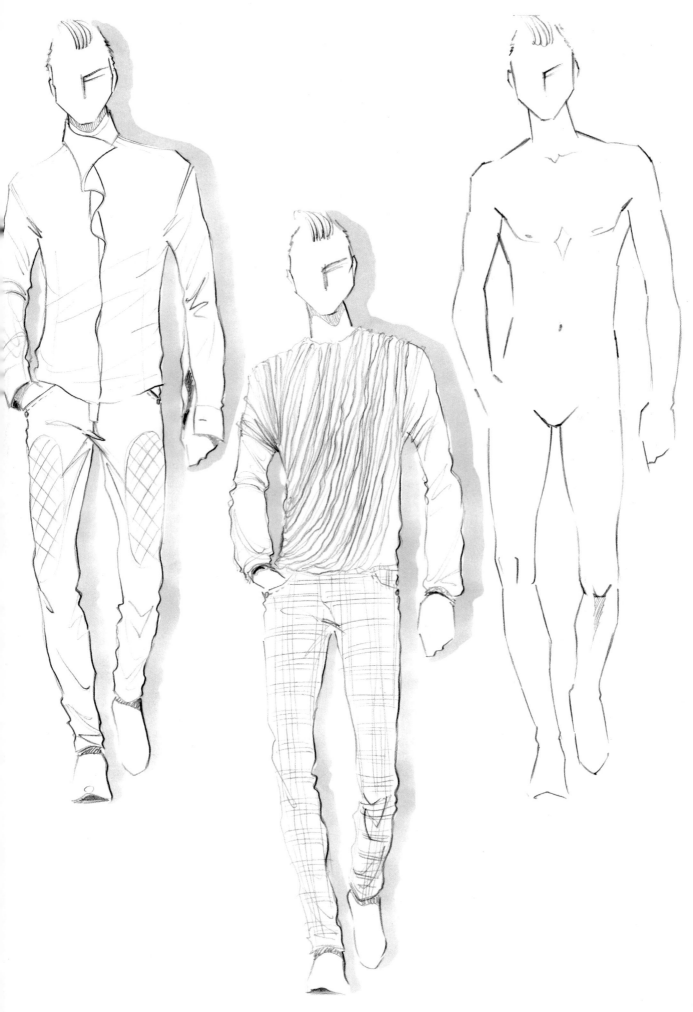

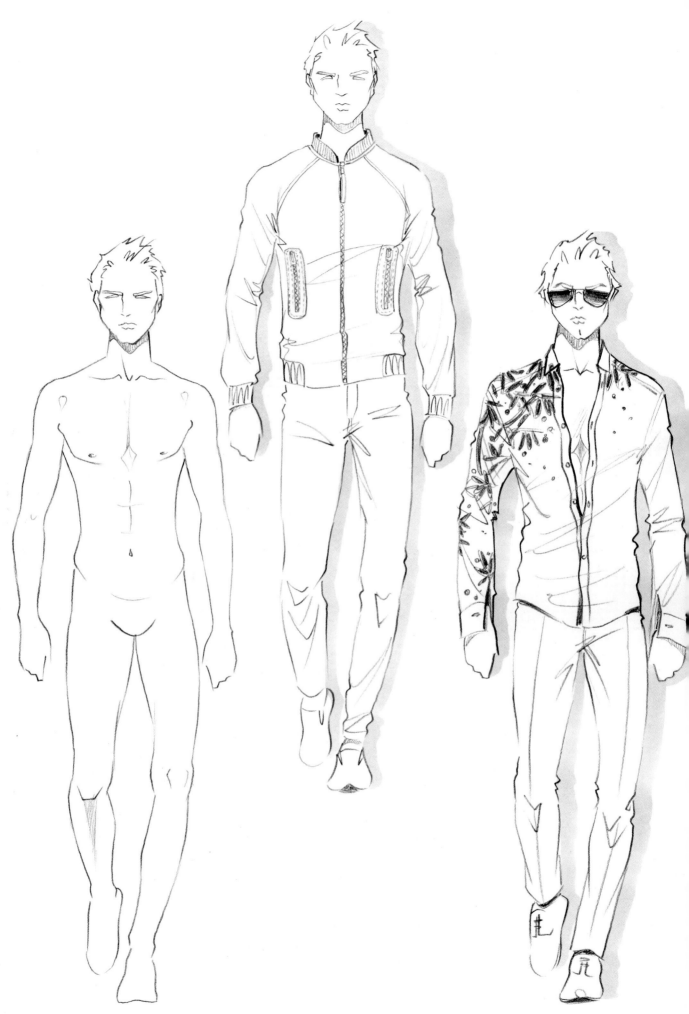

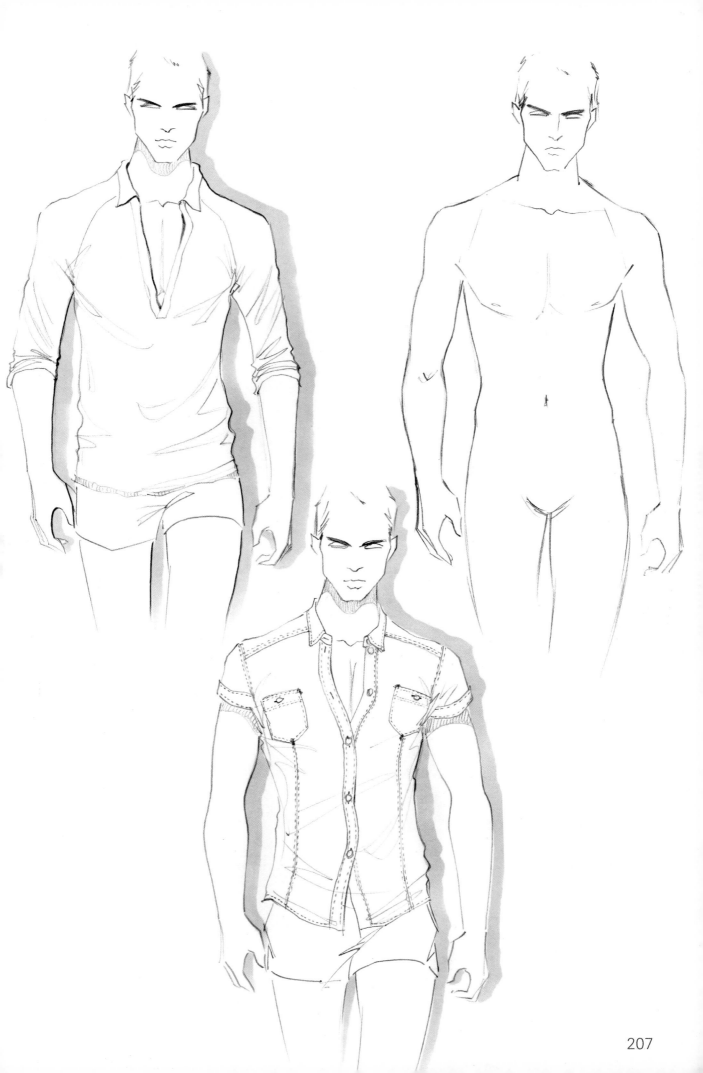

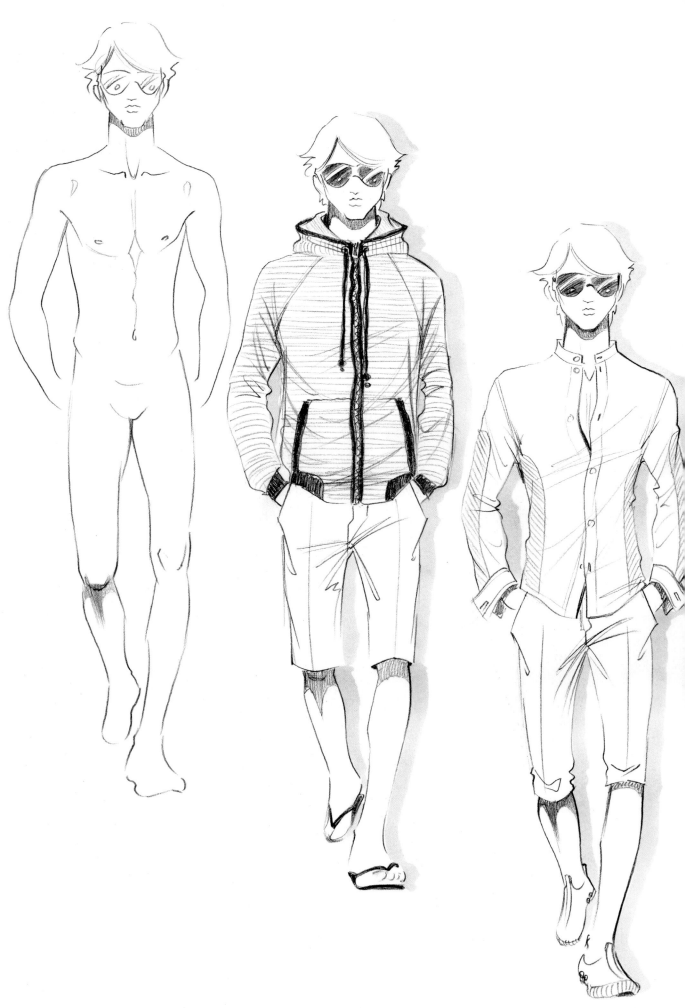

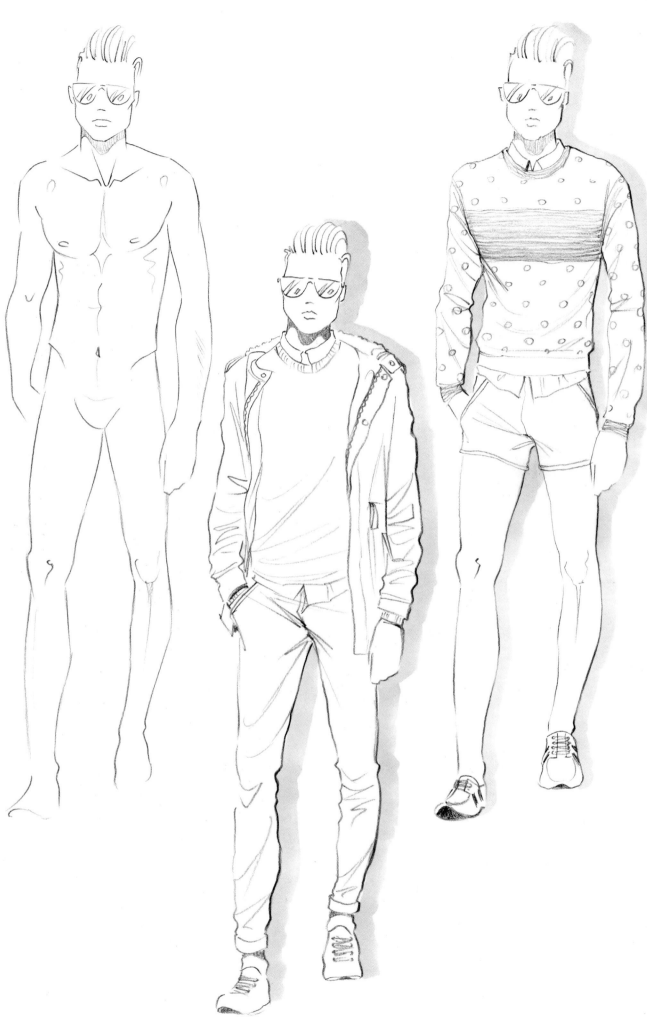

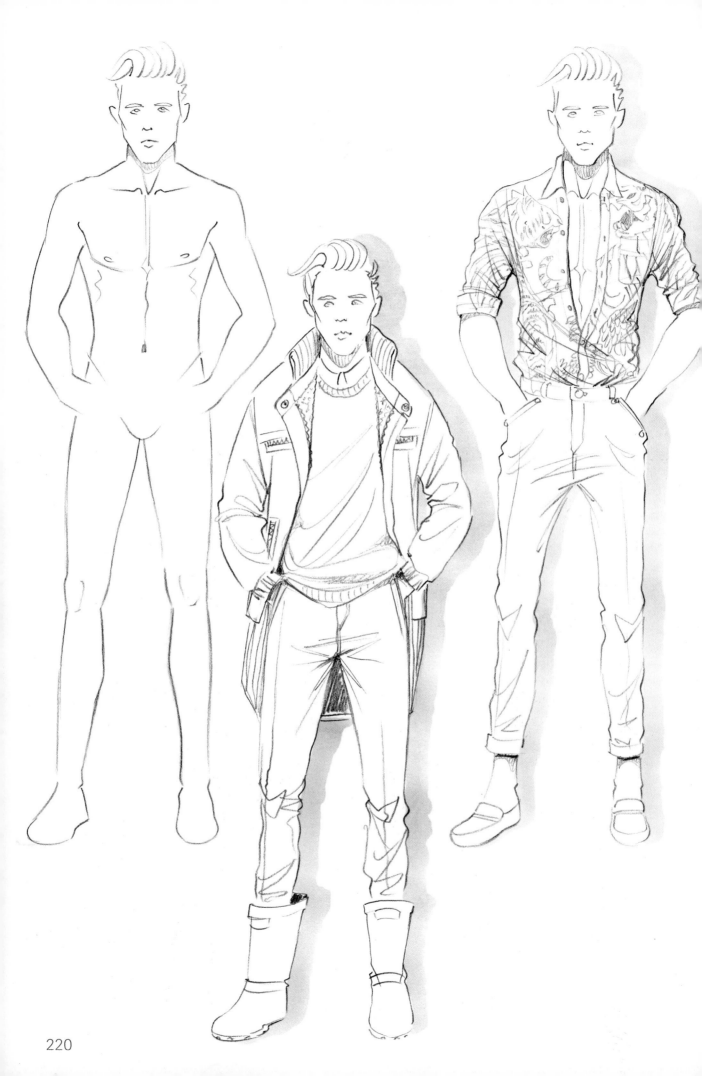

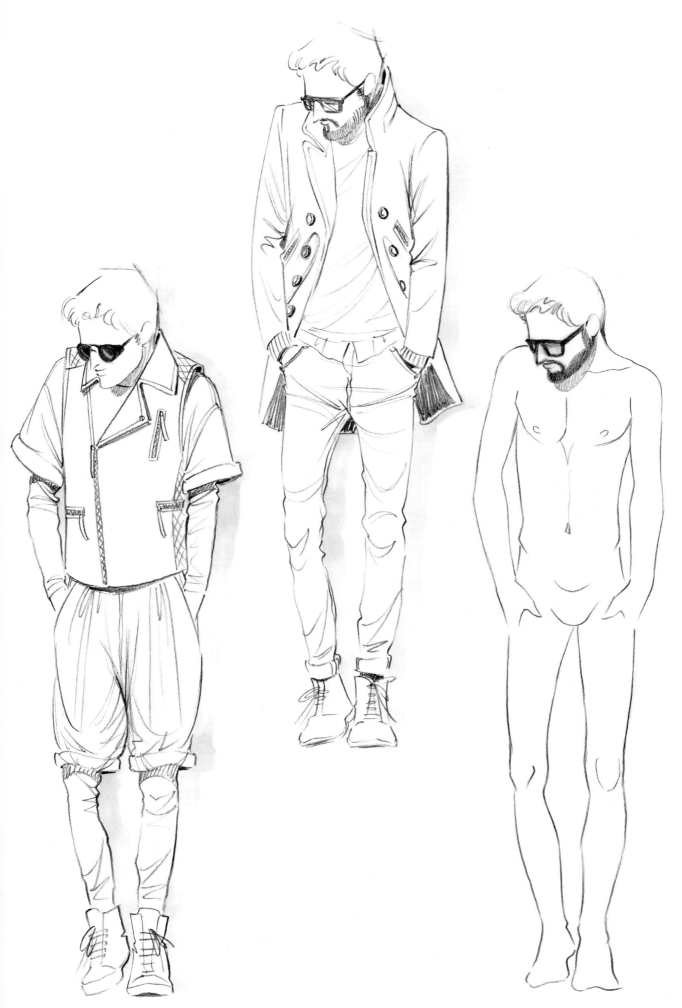

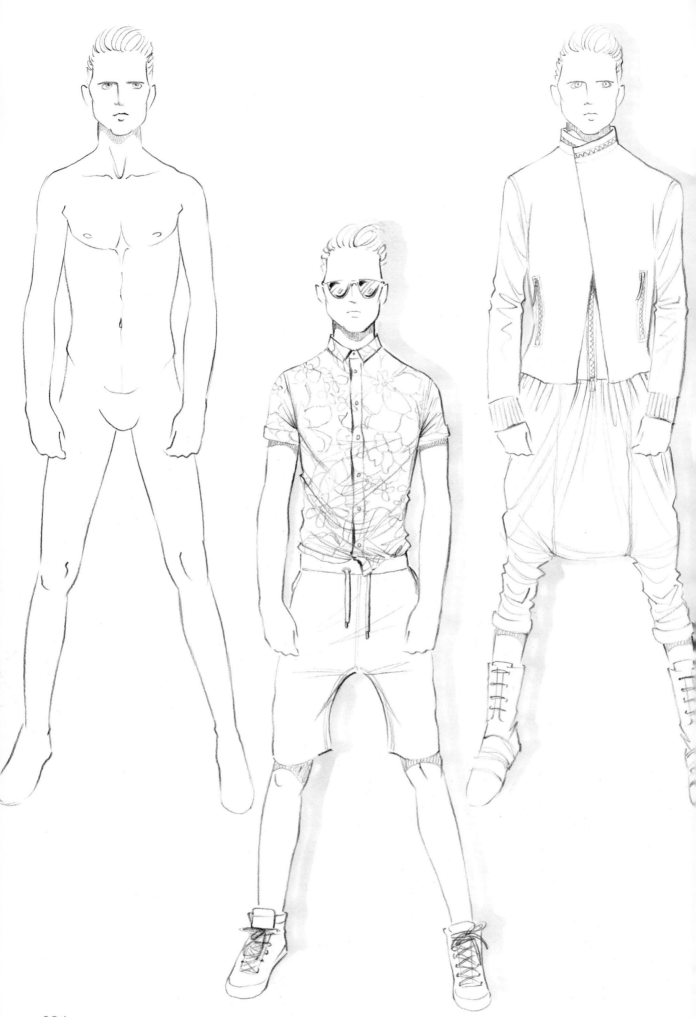

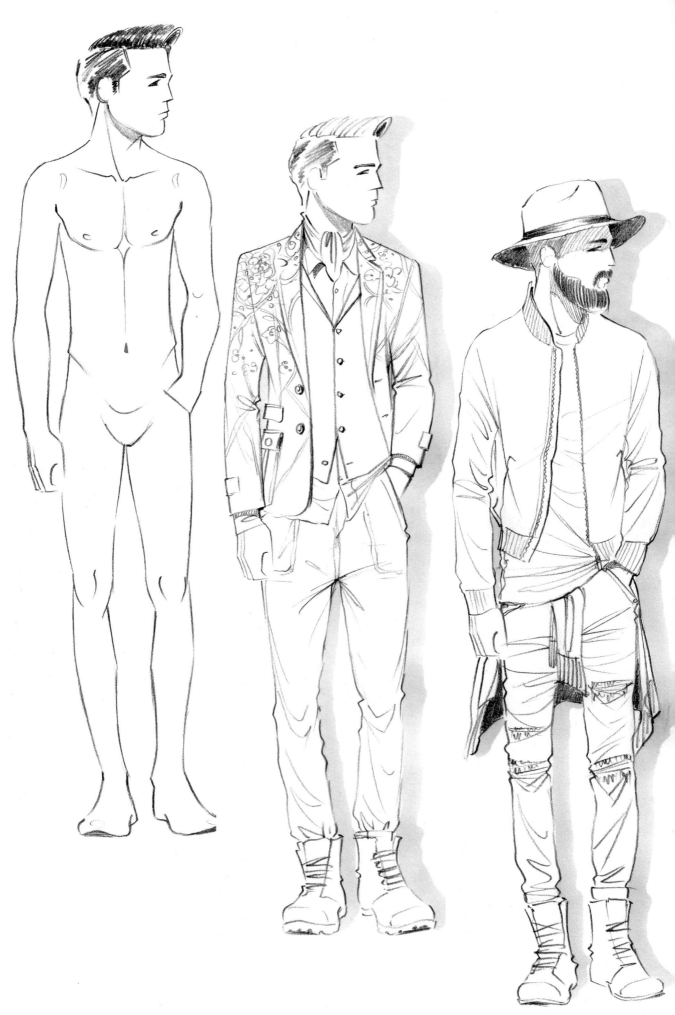

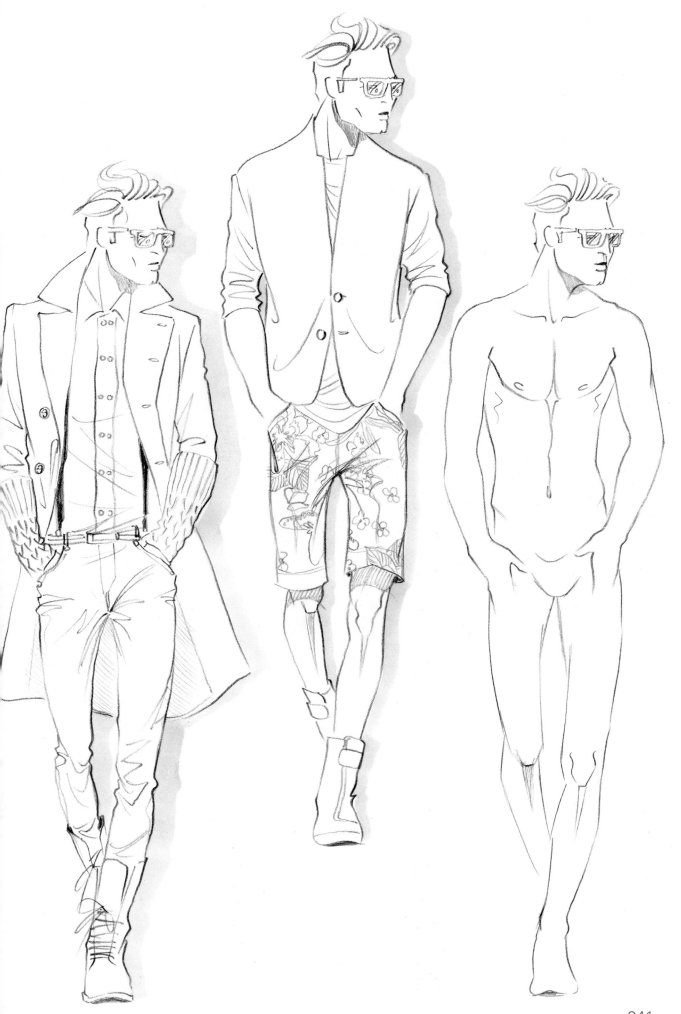

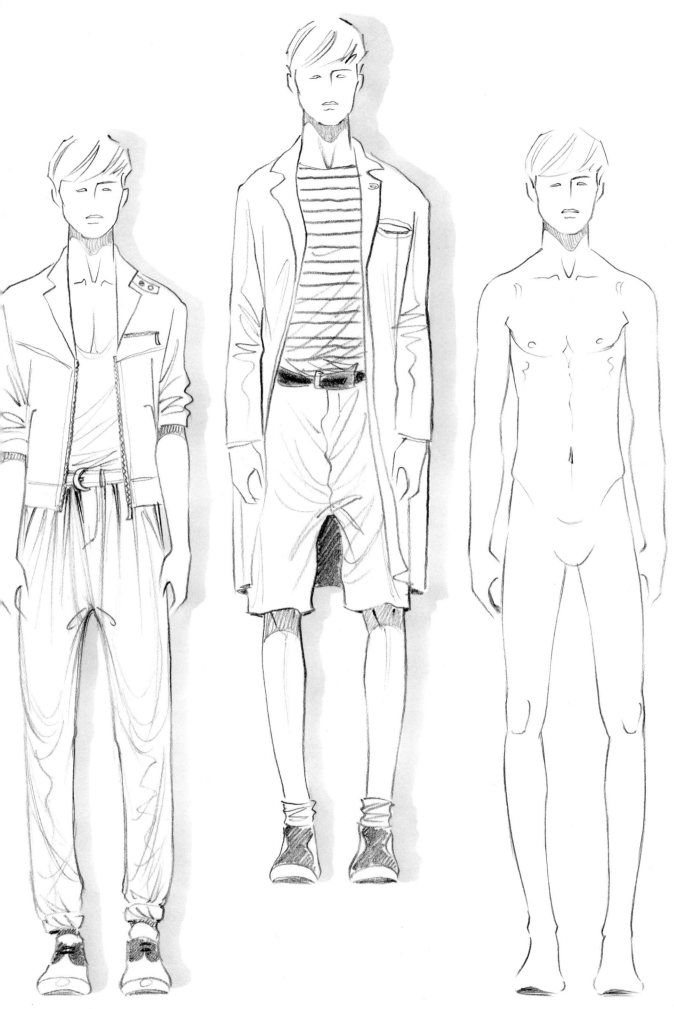

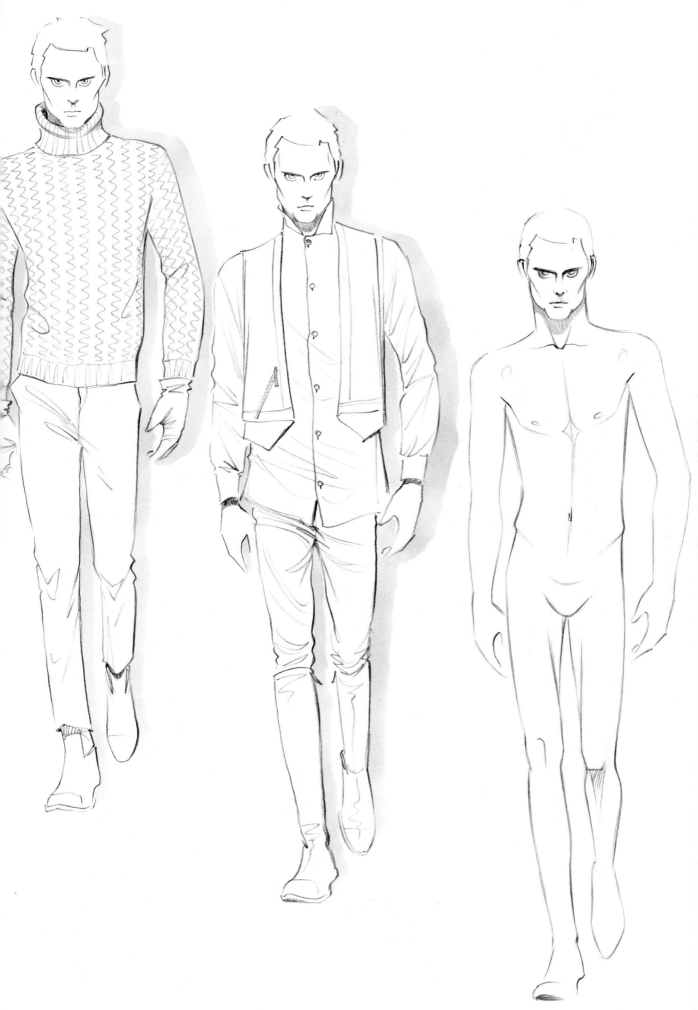

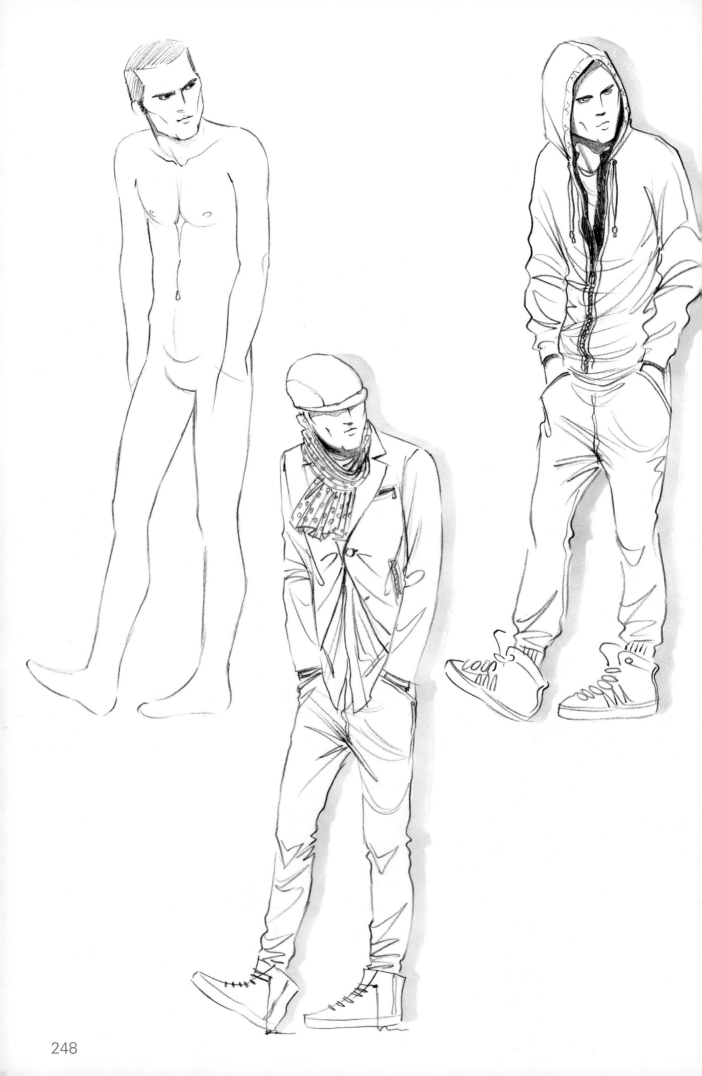

P. 214

P. 219

P. 254

P. 215

P. 227

P. 238

P. 202

P. 234

P. 250

P. 246

P. 249

P. 244

P. 243

P. 240

P. 234   P. 255   P. 239

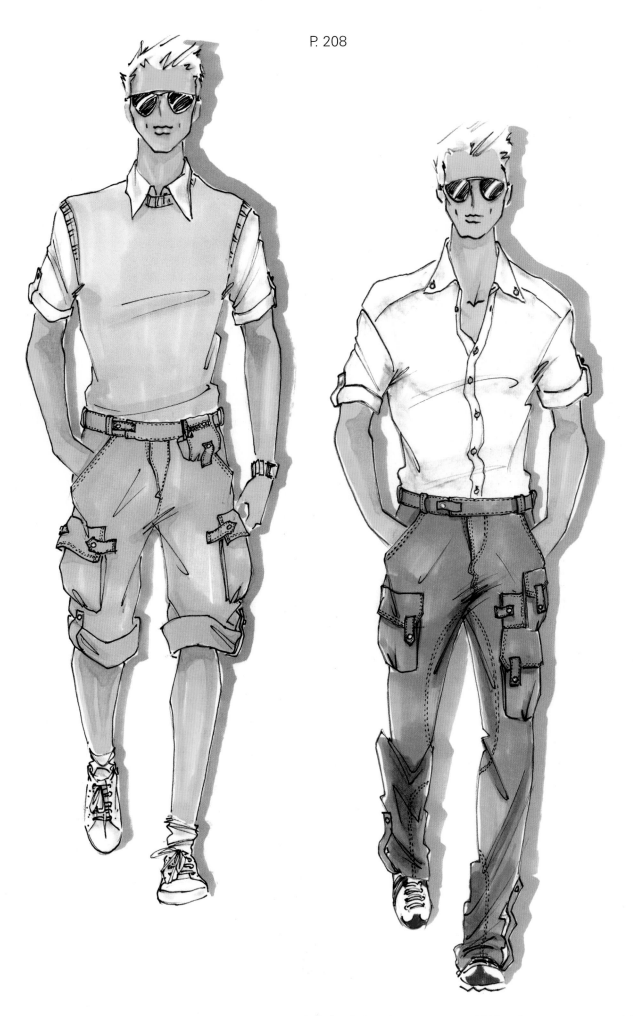

P. 252

P. 233

P. 228

P. 215

P. 230

P. 205